Luis Rua Sanchez
Juan Giler Basurto

Social Work in Health, Education and Gerontology

Luis Rua Sanchez
Juan Giler Basurto

Social Work in Health, Education and Gerontology

An inclusive approach, from different professional perspectives

ScienciaScripts

Imprint
Any brand names and product names mentioned in this book are subject to trademark, brand or patent protection and are trademarks or registered trademarks of their respective holders. The use of brand names, product names, common names, trade names, product descriptions etc. even without a particular marking in this work is in no way to be construed to mean that such names may be regarded as unrestricted in respect of trademark and brand protection legislation and could thus be used by anyone.

Cover image: www.ingimage.com

This book is a translation from the original published under ISBN 978-620-0-42384-9.

Publisher:
Sciencia Scripts
is a trademark of
International Book Market Service Ltd., member of OmniScriptum Publishing Group
17 Meldrum Street, Beau Bassin 71504, Mauritius
Printed at: see last page
ISBN: 978-620-2-70681-0

Content

This chapter intends to involve the reader in a field of action that prioritizes the Social Worker from different areas of intervention, with a humanistic sense, based on work experience and the incorporation of scientific means that generalize their action in different fields of intervention, applying techniques and instruments that allow an adequate performance in the phases that each action requires.

Although the figure of the professional in Social Work has been for years linked to charity and welfare, action that over time has highlighted the importance of the professional in institutions where social action is required as a fundamentalism for a comprehensive welfare, with the implementation of social policies that undoubtedly improve the quality of life of workers.

HEALTH SOCIAL WORKER

The fundamental objective of Social Work is to improve people's well-being, applying their scientific knowledge to this end. To this end, it is important to mention that it must begin by finding the balance of biopsychosocial factors in an effective manner, which will allow contributing to the social well-being of the context in which each individual performs.

The health system operates structurally on two levels; primary health care and specialized care, the first corresponding to that carried out in health centres, medical dispensaries of the health network, sub health centres and pre-ambulatory care. The second level of care requires a higher level of medical equipment and professionals developed in hospitals of the public health network.

At the different levels, the performance of the Social Work professional is important since it is related to the patient/user care service that requires services. According to what has been exposed by (Fernandez García & Ponce de Leon, 2014) They indicate that "the Social Worker usually carries out an assessment and a social diagnosis of the sick person and designs a psychosocial treatment that completes the process of restoring health". In this sense, effective care should be understood as a complement to the comprehensive and integrative care provided by health institutions, as indicated (Pan American Health Organization, 2008) who mentions Integrated and Comprehensive Care which states that" means that the range of services available should be sufficient to respond to the health needs of the population, including the provision of promotion, prevention, early diagnosis, cure, rehabilitation, palliative care and support for self-care. Comprehensiveness is a function of the entire health system and includes prevention, primary, secondary, tertiary and palliative care. It is important to indicate that this complete system works in a way that integrates support with the health policies of the governments, who take actions to minimize the effects that a "bad health system" could cause.

THE SOCIAL WORKER IN THE DISABILITY RATING DEPARTMENT

As people with disabilities are vulnerable, they require attention from professionals who improve their living conditions, based on permanent inclusion, with the delivery of equipment or instruments that contribute to personal and integral performance, with institutions that carry out the respective and adequate follow-up according to the World Health Organization - WHO (2011), "more than one billion people in the world, most of them elderly and disabled people, need one or more technical aids, among them two hundred million present difficulties as they age, also in the case of people with disabilities".

Taking into account that the main priority is complete balance, WHO (1946), defines health as "a state of complete physical, mental and social well-being, and not merely the absence of disease or infirmity". In other words, for an individual to enjoy complete well-being it is necessary to have a balance between all the components mentioned above by the WHO, however, the social coverage that these mean in people must be estimated, in addition to the intervention of the professional in Social Work.

The performance of the professional in the qualification department, contributes significantly to the welfare of people, to be part of the intervention process to minimize those needs more personal and the environment in which they operate, this involves carrying out a job, always within an interdisciplinary team.

In order to describe the role of the Social Work professional whose focus is on the technical aid processes of the Ministry of Public Health's disability program, several conceptual and characteristic approaches are made beforehand on essential aspects of this research, such as What is disability? and What is technical aid?

The first of these, disability, according to the United Nations Convention (2006), states that "it is an evolving concept resulting from the interaction between persons with impairments and attitudinal and environmental barriers that hinders their full and effective participation in society on an equal basis with others".

It is important to mention that disability is not a limitation for those who present it, at this stage is when inclusion links must be established that allow social equality without barriers that minimize the participation of these people, because in a society where social inequality predominates, these people must be included within the priorities of the State to improve their situation of vulnerability.

The United Nations Convention on the Rights of Persons with Disabilities (2016), in article 25, mentions that "States Parties recognize that persons with disabilities have the right to the enjoyment of the highest attainable standard of health without discrimination on the basis of disability. However, they are losing autonomy in several areas of life and the need is increasing proportionately as a result of the progressive ageing of the world's population and the increasing prevalence of diseases.

In the second conceptual approach, reference is made to what is technical aid, and therefore it was considered pertinent to mention what was stated by (Blanco, 2017) who expressed that "technical aids or support devices are products, instruments, equipment or systems used to maintain people's personal autonomy. They are manufactured and available in the market, to prevent, compensate, diminish or neutralize an impairment or disability of the person". In this sense, technical aids, which are adaptations or self-help devices, should not be confused with technical means, which are transformations carried out in the habitat, tending to eliminate the barriers that marginalise and exclude the person with a disability.

In Ecuador, according to the study carried out by the National Council for Equality of Disabilities (2020), 483,019 people have disabilities of some kind. Of these, 10,053 people have disabilities in the province of Manabí, in the canton of Portoviejo. Thus, to ensure the welfare of this priority group of attention, the National Government, through the Ministry of Public Health (MSP), is responsible for the distribution of technical aids, which include wheelchairs, bath chairs, canes, anti-eschar cushions and crutches among others, which allow families that have qualified members with some kind of disability to mobilize them and integrate them into the family context, which become indispensable at the time of establishing communication with users, because they reflect the importance of maintaining direct contact with them.

Given the conditions that preceded this research, the importance of the intervention of the Social Work professional in the different processes of action with the individuals that present a need that involves social inclusion in the different programs destined to people with disabilities is detected. By virtue of that, the objective of this research is to analyze the role of the Social Worker in the processes of technical aids of the disability program of the Ministry of Public Health.

Health can be understood in a double dimension: as a product of the social and biological conditions in which the human being is immersed; and at the same time as a producer of situations that allow integral development at an individual and collective level, it is built within the framework of economic, social, political, cultural and environmental conditions, and of the forms of relationship with social groups.

People with disabilities, being vulnerable, require these conditions that allow them to be included in society, which guarantees the same opportunities in the different fields of action, that is, they require attention from professionals who improve their living conditions, based on permanent inclusion, with the delivery of equipment or instruments that contribute to personal and integral performance, with institutions that carry out the corresponding follow-up.

According to (Reds, 2017) A Social Worker is "a professional who dedicates his or her career to the service of people in a situation of social risk and who seeks to help them in a direct way or in a preventive way by means of the elaboration of plans and interventions, in order to act on the causes that are generating this situation, but this is not limited to acting, but rather to a group of functions".

The action of the professional is to minimize at all times the social problems that affect the user who goes to the institutions in search of improving their current condition, where the Social Worker intervenes in conjunction with the interdisciplinary team applying different instruments that allow the diagnosis of the real situation that the individual suffers, this can be in the socio-economic context, prior to obtaining technical assistance, following the principles outlined by (English, 2014)who mentions that "human worth must be recognized, without distinction as to race, economic status, religion, political opinion or conduct. A sense of dignity and self-respect must be fostered in man." (p. 91-92).

In this context, Executive Decree 1188 of July 7, 2001, was (2008)In order to improve the quality of life of people with disabilities, a national information system was implemented, detailing the type of disability and percentage, socio-economic status and other needs encountered. This system established the priorities of people with disabilities and allowed all public and private institutions to take immediate action to improve their infrastructure in an inclusive manner.

In this sense, it is organized for the distribution of goods, including health services, and how these conditions are processed at the individual level and on a biological and spiritual basis, as mentioned in the Guide for the Care of Persons with Disabilities in Rural Health (2015)He states that "Health as a producer of development implies a conscious effort by individuals and social groups, based on the improvement of living conditions, the generation of opportunities, acquires a role of social cohesion and can be constituted in the process of social development", so that an adequate condition in the state of health, allows to reach a harmony in the social environment and contributes to strengthen the psychosocial state of individuals, who need these conditions to make viable an adequate quality of life that accompanies the circumstantial improvement of the immediate environment.

LEGAL REGULATION FRAMEWORK

According to the Constitution of the Republic of Ecuador (2008)Article 35 states that "Older persons, children and adolescents, pregnant women, persons with disabilities, persons deprived of liberty and those suffering from catastrophic or highly complex diseases shall receive priority and specialized attention in the public and private spheres. The same priority attention will be given to persons at risk, victims of domestic and sexual violence, child abuse, and natural or man-made disasters. The State shall provide special protection to persons in a situation of double vulnerability.

Considering the previous article, the Ecuadorian State must guarantee priority attention to improve the quality of life of vulnerable people, taking actions that allow inclusion and respect for their rights. As stated in article 48 of the Ecuadorian Constitution, "The State shall adopt measures in favour of persons with disabilities that ensure

Paragraph 5 mentions the establishment of specialized programmes for the comprehensive care of persons with severe and profound disabilities, in order to achieve the maximum development of their personality, the promotion of their autonomy and the reduction of dependence".

The programs that allow the inclusion of people with disabilities are established at a national level, these are focused on comprehensive care, with an interdisciplinary team that makes home visits when users have some situation that does not allow them to mobilize. Article 226 of the Constitution of the Republic provides that: "State institutions, their agencies, dependencies, civil servants and persons acting under a State authority shall exercise only the powers and competences assigned to them by the Constitution and the law. They shall have the duty to coordinate actions for the fulfilment of their purposes and to make effective the enjoyment and exercise of the rights recognized in the Constitution.

The Organic Law on Disability (2012) in the second section of the national subsystem for the qualification of disability, in article 9. "The national health authority, through the National Health System, shall carry out the qualification of disabilities and the continuous training of the qualifying teams specialized in the various types of disabilities that will exercise their functions in the area of their specialty. The qualification of the disability to determine its type, level or percentage will be carried out at the request of the interested party, of the person who represents him/her or of the persons or entities that are in his/her charge; which will be voluntary, personalized and free. In the case of Ecuadorians residing abroad, the qualification of disability will be made through diplomatic representations in accordance with the regulations. The national health authority shall train and accredit, in accordance with the Act and the regulations, technical and specialized personnel in classification, assessment and methods for the qualification of the condition of disability;

Article 1.- Extend the validity of the "CONADIS disability card" until June 30, 2021; and, extend the validity of the "Ministry of Public Health - MSP disability card" until June 30, 2023, as established in the schedule attached to this resolution.

The National Council for Equality of Disabilities (CONADIS) and the Ministry of Public Health (MSP), through the Manuela Espejo Mission, are the qualifying institutions for the delivery of these aids, which make viable and execute the delivery to people with disabilities throughout the country, and specifically in the cantons of Manta, Pedernales, Chone, Jama, Rocafuerte and Portoviejo; who were affected by the earthquake of April 16.

TYPES OF TECHNICAL AIDS

According to the WHO (2016)The list of priority technical aids is a reference for the development of coherent national policies and programmes on priority assistive technologies that could help change this situation and facilitate access to technical aids worldwide". Indeed, the Ecuadorian State is complying with the adaptation and delivery of support tools for people with disabilities, so that in the Department of Qualification of Disability of the Andrés de Vera health center in the canton of Portoviejo, the following technical aids are granted:

- ✓ **WHEELCHAIRS:** This is a means of transporting people with walking limitations. It is used as a technical aid to be able to transport a patient by pushing or to allow a person with limitation to reach places or services needed.

- ✓ URINE-ABRASING **PRODUCTS:** These are items that absorb urine, such as adult diapers, plastic-covered underwear, sanitary pads, or day pads that attach to underwear. Most items for sale are disposable. Some absorbent clothing can be washed and reused. There are also drip collectors that are placed over the penis

- ✓ **ANTI-SHOCK MATTRESSES:** It is a special surface that distributes the weight of the body, relieving the pressure and thus avoiding the appearance of the dreaded bedsores that appear on the skin due to immobility.

- ✓ **TREKKERS:** These are orthopaedic devices that allow you to walk while leaning on them and on your extremities. They considerably increase the support base and, therefore, the stability and balance of the patient. It is also important to point out that they provide great psychological security to the patient who uses them, since he or she loses the fear of falling.

- ✓ **MULTIPODAL POLE:** Usually used by geriatric patients who have suffered hip fractures, lower limb amputations to start walking, hemiplegics, lower limb amputees and patients with severe paralytic sequelae.

- ✓ **MULETS:** These are orthopaedic devices that allow a direct support on the trunk, which provides great stability and balance, leaving your hands free at the same time. In general, patients accept them with great difficulty. Nowadays, they are in disuse because they are not very aesthetic. To perform the pendulum walk

Canes, like crutches, serve to facilitate walking by increasing stability, i.e., this allows for a larger support base and/or a reduced load on one or both lower extremities. The poles are made of wood or aluminium and are adjustable in height. They are the simplest walking aids and, for this reason, tend to be forgotten in the early care of people who need help in the initial stages of their walking disability. In fact, when a patient is suggested to use a cane, he very often rejects it as a sign of senility or disability. They are indicated in functional deficits of one or both lower extremities caused by musculoskeletal or neurological pathology.

When the deficits are very important, crutches will be preferred to canes, and if the upper limbs are affected it will be necessary to modify them. Simple canes are unstable if forces greater than 20-25% of the body weight are applied to them. Their main function is to provide balance and increase the feeling of stability. If greater support and stability is required, crutches should be used, primarily for forearm support.

All of these implements are mostly given to people with disabilities with a high rate of poverty, in compensation for the social policies of governments in their struggle to improve access and permanent inclusion of people with disabilities, allowing them to share in an inclusive context both in the family and individual.

METHODOLOGY USED

The development and management of this research was based on a qualitative approach according to (Juan Baez and Perez de Tudela, 2014) They mention that it is aligned with empiricism in its most general form, while knowledge is obtained as a consequence of experience, it is direct knowledge, not mediated, because it is produced in situ, the bibliographical method was also used which according to (University of Valencia , 2017) indicates that it integrates the accounts of a whole life or of certain stages or biographical events of relevance to the person studied, in addition to all the information or documents that may be available about the life of the subject of study, with the purpose of knowing and analyzing the perception of the social reality of the person studied and descriptive that according to (Marroquin, 2012) Also known as statistical research, the data and characteristics of the population or phenomenon under study are described. This level of Research answers the questions: who, what, where, when and how. The technique of the interview was applied and as instrument the guide of interview, directed to the professional of the department of qualification of disability of the district of health Andres de Vera of the canton Portoviejo.

RESULTS

According to the National Agenda for Disability Equality (2017)In order to qualify and accredit persons with disabilities throughout the national territory, the Ministry of Health has set up 281 disability qualification teams, comprising 729 medical professionals, psychologists and social workers, in 175 cantons of the country, who are responsible for establishing the corresponding types, degrees and percentages of disability. The qualifications are entered in an administrative register, called the National Disability Register, for the respective issuance of the disability card.

The bibliographic review carried out in this research is complemented with the information obtained through the interview with the Social Worker of the Disability Qualification Department of the Andrés de Vera Health Center. Through this technique, it was possible to identify the significant work performed by this professional, who acts in accordance with the regulatory framework established in the Constitution of the Republic of Ecuador (2008) and the Organic Law on Disabilities.

It is considered important to mention that people who require the qualification of disability, granted by the Ministry of Public Health must perform a series of actions that are regulated by the national health authority, which is the only entity empowered to grant qualification to these users. Regarding the granting of technical aids that are carried out in the department of qualification of the Andres de Vera Health Center of the Portoviejo Canton, the process contemplates nine stages, which are established below:

1. The user or family member must call the 171 options 4 toll-free line to schedule an appointment for disability qualification from the Ministry of Public Health.

2. At the call center, the applicant's ID number will be requested, and the home address will be confirmed, for the availability of the qualifying health center, closest to the user.

3. A shift is scheduled immediately within 24 to 48 hours maximum.

4. The user is asked to attend the qualifying health center 30 minutes before, to open the medical history and other complementary requirements.

5. The user must carry the form 001, issued by the specialist, in which the current situation and the need for the appraisal are corroborated.

6. Within the biopsychosocial intervention carried out on the user, the social worker carries out a social assessment of the family's socioeconomic situation, in which the professional issues a maximum weighting of 10 points. In conjunction with the medical appraiser who determines the percentage according to the difficulty presented.

7. The disability card is issued with the percentages established by the qualifying team

8. According to the user's needs, technical assistance is requested by means of the prescription form.

9. The requested help is delivered immediately if it is available, otherwise the user or family member must return to the centre within 15 days.

ROLE OF THE SOCIAL WORKER IN THE DISABILITY RATING DEPARTMENT

In this order of ideas the professional in Social Work of the department of qualification of Disability manifested that they carry out a work together with the medical team for the respective intervention, considering that if the user with family help goes to the Department of qualification of Disability:

Previously it receives the medical evaluation, which allows to determine the acquisition of the card, then it is derived to the social worker so that it carries out a socioeconomic study, applying the matrix of updated Scale, in this it evaluates the socioeconomic level, and the existing resources in the familiar surroundings of the user, this matrix is structured with a weighting of 15 points, the result of this evaluation at social level, are fundamental for the emission of the card.

It should be noted that there are cases in which users cannot mobilize the qualification department by their own means, since a home visit is made in conjunction with the medical, psychological and social worker staff, the latter intervening by applying a daily part, which allows them to collect information for the relevant management, In addition, the Baremo social assessment matrix is applied, which identifies relevant aspects at the individual, family, economic and social   level of the user. This in turn provides a maximum score that is established by the professional and which is added to the general percentage assigned by the other members of the interdisciplinary team.

Later, the respective card is issued with the confirmed data, the respective percentage and the disability it presents, said document is delivered within a period of 15 days, then the Social Worker fills out a technical aid prescription form, which indicates the type of implement requested prior to the medical observations, In the case of not having this implement in the center, the request is made to the Zonal Health Coordination, and when these are available, the user is contacted so that a relative can come and pick it up, with the original identity document and the card respectively.

SCIENTIFIC CONTRIBUTIONS

The professional performance of the Social Worker generates in the users that space of confidence to expose their problems, where there is a necessary approach to receive important information in the search for solutions. According to Gómez (2016), "The Social Worker has become a fundamental pillar in the institutions that require his or her contribution. Before, the role of the professional was very scarce and at the same time absent, but as the years have passed and the new change in society has taken place, this professional's presence has become something useful".

Continuing with this analysis, the author believes that the role of the social worker is fundamental in health services because it allows them to know more about the users who require technical aids for their improvement.

With respect to technical aids, they represent a welfare in people with disabilities, who when using them tend to feel included by the institutions of the state, who grant them these instruments, even (Melo, 2019), states that: "the objective of these programs is to develop the actions of integral attention, through the granting of devices of assistance people according to the characteristics and individual needs of people with disabilities, their family, caretaker or caregiver in order to improve their habits in their lifestyles".

The attention of these people who present difficulties, requires a whole interdisciplinary team who, by means of interventions, allow to diagnose the current situation, economic condition, the causes for which they cannot buy these implements because of their high cost. Similarly, the (Fundación Once, 2018) states that "The aids or benefits are intended to help with the expenses derived from acquisitions or adaptations, and also include the repairs or maintenance of some aids".

As a whole, these implements, being granted by an agency responsible for the health of citizens, do not require any intervention prior to use, as stated (Pinedo, 2017), "support products do not include any type of medical rehabilitation element or requiring surgical intervention for use, and must always be directly related to the disability of the applicant.

Each instrument is in accordance with the difficulty presented by the applicant, that is, it is appropriate according to the qualifications received by the medical professional who evaluates the condition prior to its use, who in some cases requires a home visit due to the difficulty of mobilizing the applicant, as stated by the (Ministry of Economic and Social Inclusion, 2018) "This aid reaches people with disabilities through a previous technical visit in their homes. This first approach allows to verify their real needs and thus be able to deliver the necessary equipment, to improve the quality of life".

CONCLUSION

The Social Worker carries out his professional work in the health field, in a systemic way promoting changes and transformations in the personal, collective and social dynamics that lead to the construction of improvements in the lifestyles of people with disabilities who lack the necessary tools to improve their living conditions.

The technical aids represent a vital instrument in the improvement of the living conditions of people with disabilities, allowing them to believe in the possibilities of continuing a process of adaptability and personal improvement, giving confidence in themselves which raises self-esteem and vitalises family relationships, allowing consecutive interaction within the family.

Technical aids such as personal aids play a crucial role in achieving equal opportunities for people with disabilities in different facets of life, because they provide some compensation for disability-related functional limitations and increase the chances of inclusion that is implemented in a comprehensive manner, without limitation to this priority group.

The Social Worker is prepared to exercise his work in the field of health, intervening in people with disabilities who require this professional intervention, which significantly improves their living conditions, prior to the process that is carried out in the social assessment carried out by the professional.

Bibliography Used

National Agenda for Equality of Disabilities. (2017). *Planificacion.gob.* Retrieved from https://www.planificacion.gob.ec/wp-content/uploads/downloads/2018/08/Agenda-Nacional-para-Discapacidades.pdf

Barriers, E. s. (October 14, 2008). *Zero Latitude.* Retrieved from https://www.cerolatitud.ec/direccion-distrital-17d02-salud-realiza-acciones-constantes-beneficio-las-personas-discapacidad/

Blanco, C. (06 of 06 of 2017). *Gila.* Retrieved from https://www.ela.org.mx/2017/06/que-son-las-ayudas-tecnicas-y-para-que-sirven/

Castellanos, M. (2014). *Social Work: Characteristics, principles, objectives and functions.* Madrid: Profars.

National Council for Equality of Disabilities. (20 February 2020). Disability *Council.* Retrieved from https://www.consejodiscapacidades.gob.ec/estadisticas-de-discapacidad/

Constitution of the Republic of Ecuador. (October 20, 2008). *Oas.* Obtained from https://www.oas.org/juridico/pdfs/mesicic4_ecu_const.pdf

United Nations Convention on the Rights of Persons with Disabilities (2006). *Ministry of Health of Colombia.* Retrieved from https://www.minsalud.gov.co/Documentos%20y%20Publicaciones/Convenci%C3%B3n%20sobre%20los%20Derechos%20de%20las%20Personas%20con%20Discapacidad%20Protocolo%20Facultativo.pdf

United Nations Convention on the Rights of Persons with Disabilities (2016). *Physical Disability Observatory.* Retrieved from https://www.observatoridiscapacitat.org/es/discapacidad-y-salud

Fernandez García, T., & Ponce de Leon, L. (2014). *Nociones Basicas de Trabajo Social.* Madrid, Spain: Ediciones Académicas.

Foundation Eleven. (July 4, 2018). *Discapnet.* Retrieved from https://www.discapnet.es/areas-tematicas/derechos/prestaciones-subvenciones/otras-prestaciones/ayudas-tecnicas

Gomez, R. (October 12, 2016). *University of Machala.* Retrieved from http://repositorio.utmachala.edu.ec/bitstream/48000/8173/1/TTUACS%20DE00003.pdf

Guide to care for people with disabilities in rural health. (2015). *Ministry of Public Health of Ecuador.* Retrieved from https://bibliotecapromocion.msp.gob.ec/greenstone/collect/promocin/index/assoc/HASH4f82.dir/doc.pdf

Juan Baez and Perez de Tudela. (2014). *eprints.* (J. M. Merino, Ed.) Retrieved from https://eprints.ucm.es/29615/1/T35974.pdf

Organic Disabilities Act. (September 25, 2012). Disabilities *Council.* Retrieved from https://www.consejodiscapacidades.gob.ec/wp-content/uploads/downloads/2014/02/ley_organica_discapacidades.pdf

Marroquin, R. (2012). *National University of Education Enrique Guzman y Valle* . Retrieved from http://www.une.edu.pe/Sesion04-Metodologia_de_la_investigacion.pdf

Melo, S. (May 22, 2019). *Bogota.* Retrieved from https://bogota.gov.co/mi-ciudad/ayudas-tecnicas-para-personas-con-discapacidad-en-bogota

Ministry of Economic and Social Inclusion. (August 10, 2018). *MIESS.* Retrieved from https://www.inclusion.gob.ec/personas-con-discapacidad-reciben-ayudas-tecnicas-en-el-guasmo-sur-de-guayaquil/

World Health Organization. (22 July 1946). *World Health Organization.* Retrieved from https://www.who.int/es/about/who-we-are/frequently-asked-questions

World Health Organization. (2011). *Who International* . Retrieved from https://www.who.int/disabilities/world_report/2011/es/

Pan American Health Organization. (2008). *Paho.* Retrieved from Pan American Health Organization : https://www.paho.org/hq/dmdocuments/2010/APS-Estrategias_Desarrollo_Equipos_APS.pdf

Pinedo, M. (March 17, 2017). *The Swan.* Retrieved from https://elcisne.org/ayudas-tecnicas-para-personas-con-discapacidad/

Rojas, C. (January 6, 2017). *Iplacex.* Retrieved from https://www.iplacex.cl/blog/los-distintos-roles-de-un-trabajador-social

Health, O. M. (2016). *World Health Organization.* Retrieved from https://apps.who.int/iris/bitstream/handle/10665/207697/WHO_EMP_PHI_2016.01_spa.pdf;jsessionid=9DFE6F9C097EE4BC82EE07E81BDC5142?sequence=1

University of Valencia . (2017). University of *Valencia* . Retrieved from https://www.uv.es/innopfg/el_mtodo_biogrfico.html

SECOND CHAPTER

In this section you will find in a technical way the actions carried out by the social work professional from different sources of action; on one hand a gerontological level and on the other an educational level.

This conception will allow the reader to get involved from a different perspective based on institutional experience, actions and mechanisms with which they intervene to reduce problems on different social fronts

ROLE OF THE SOCIAL WORKER AT THE GERONTOLOGICAL CENTRE GUILLERMINA LOOR DE MORENO

From the beginning, the career of Social Work is characterized by systematizing the categories presented in problems to develop own and appropriate models of intervention that streamline any social protocol and maximize personal, group, family and community welfare. Over the years, the Social Worker has adapted to the changes obtained in a contemporary society through globalization. This means that in the emergence of new conflicts, emergencies and badly applied bureaucratic problems, new social subjects, age groups and movements appear that need an adequate and formulated intervention. Society itself is in charge of magnifying situations that are badly led to problems that make extreme need more expensive, social policies on the one hand protect the individual in all its dimensions, however, "social" norms point to the elderly individual as an "unusable subject", "without strength" and "incompetent".

The (Organic Law on Older Persons, 2019) In the fundamental principles and provisions, article 1 states that: "The purpose of this Act is to promote, regulate and guarantee the full validity, dissemination and exercise of the specific rights of older persons, within the framework of the principle of priority and specialized attention, as expressed in the Constitution of the Republic, international human rights instruments and related laws, with a gender, human mobility, generational and intercultural approach". Article 2 of the Act states that "this Act shall apply to Ecuadorian and foreign older adults in Ecuador".

Here comes the implementation and application of public policy, as well as in the technical instruments that are generated in relation to older persons, the approaches of gender, human rights, interculturality and intergenerational should be incorporated in a mandatory way in all plans, programs and projects for their integration. In this context, residential gerontological centres are designed to accommodate those elderly people who cannot be cared for by their families or who lack a place to live permanently. They are reception services that provide care and comprehensive attention in terms of accommodation, food, nutrition, clothing, health and recreation, among others.

The Guillermina Loor de Moreno Gerontological Center currently provides timely attention with quality and warmth, by generating policies, regulations, strategies, programs and services based on the integral development of the life cycle such as: social protection, social mobility, economic inclusion, universal insurance and priority attention groups. In the field of action, the Social Worker considers the older adult as an actor of social and family development, operating, evaluating and following up the process in which the user is immersed from before he or she enters the institution, improving as much as possible the functional and mental capacity through participation in appropriate therapies and programs.

SOCIAL WORK

The Social Worker acquires integral knowledge that allows him/her to intervene at a macro-social level in the organization, direction and coordination of programs and institutions; he/she also intervenes in the planning of policies and strategies to achieve social welfare. (Castellanos, 1993). Social Work is a scientific discipline that results from evidence-based practice or vice versa, this shows that one must start from evidence to obtain a professional practice or therefore obtain the practice through scientific evidence. This profession considers important the observation of some phenomenon or fact, seeing the problem as an opportunity to favour, develop and promote social changes towards a well-being for people.

SOCIAL WORKER PRINCIPLES

- Provide priority attention through the services established by the institution.

- To improve or maintain as far as possible the functional and mental capacity of users, through participation in appropriate therapies and programs.

- Encourage self-effort as a means of developing the person's sense of self-confidence and ability to take responsibility.

- Make responsible use of the professional relationship with a view to objectively promoting the good of the user.

OBJECT OF PROFESSIONAL INTERVENTION

The professional in Social Work distinguishes the objectives that are raised in every action, plans and promotes resources to solve situations. The objectives are specific to each instrument of that planning, plan, program, project in particular, within the context of social and institutional reality, as the objectives are guidelines for decision making.

The objectives of professional intervention are guided by three fundamental lines which are

THE ORIENTATION

As a means of transmitting the information and training content necessary and required by the population. This objective can be fulfilled through the professional functions of education, awareness, training, advice and general reflection of the concrete reality faced.

ORGANIZATION

It is involved in training to understand the different and varied forms of grouping in: committees, associations, cooperatives, unions, commissions and others. It develops people's capacity to face problem situations, as well as to look for different ways of alternative solutions.

MOBILIZATION

It includes actions that the population must carry out in order to face a problem and seek relevant solutions. In other words, the professional must guide people towards the movement and use of resources, assignment of tasks, allocation of time for action, etc.

SOCIAL WORKER OBJECTIVES

To promote and participate in the tasks of research, planning, execution and scientific evaluation, both in institutions and in social welfare programs, so that their actions are an effective response to the satisfaction of needs and solutions to social problems.

2- Promote, stimulate and technically orient the social organization in the way required by the social reality, so that those affected and interested in solving their problems create adequate conditions to satisfy their needs by their own effort and cooperation, aimed at achieving their own social welfare.

3.- To critically interpret the national reality in order to contribute to the process of social transformation of the country and to participate in programmes that, while providing material solutions, allow for tasks aimed at obtaining qualitative changes.

To contribute to the introduction of changes in mentality, attitude and behaviour in individuals, groups and communities, which will make it easier for them to discover, analyse and interpret (in an objective manner) the causes that are holding back their development.

5.- To promote coordination between the different sectors that are affected, as well as the service institutions that may be public or private, thus taking advantage of human, technical, material and financial resources in the implementation of projects.

6.- Propitiate and guide the evaluation of the institutions and programs of well-being, to try that the subjects of social action are involved in this process with the purpose of placing at the height circumstances and needs of the population.

7.- Maintain attention to the participation of individual and collective rights (Declaration of Human Rights).

GERONTOLOGICAL SOCIAL WORK

Pineapple (2004) defines it as "a field of action that aims to enhance the individual, family, group and community social capital of older adults, improving the quality of their social life and their human development, through social intervention based on epistemological, theoretical and methodological approaches". That is to say, it studies the older adult in all its dimension, focusing on their areas of study to prioritize their needs based on the results obtained from an interdisciplinary approach, its purpose being to know the aging process that allows to improve the quality of life.

This is the study of old age from an interdisciplinary approach, its purpose being to optimize the aging process in order to improve the quality of life obtained during the life cycle. For this reason, the promotion of new lifestyles, social integration and socialization that generates support networks for the elderly is the focus of our professional practice. In this perspective it promotes the active aging that goes beyond the healthy aging, from the disciplinary reflection of the gerontological social work, constructed through the last decades, I consider it must already be a field of specialization since its action aims at harnessing the individual, familiar, group and communitarian social capital of the older adults, improving the quality of their social life and their personal development, through a social intervention based on epistemological, theoretical and methodological approaches that empower them to co-responsibility for the care of their autonomy and functional self-valence as a support for their participation and full exercise of their citizen rights in their social and family environment.

GERONTOLOGY

According to the (U.S. National Academy of Sciences, 2018) Gerontology is the scientific study of the processes and problems of ageing from all aspects: biological, clinical, psychological, sociological, legal, economic and political. Likewise, the (WHO, 2013) defines it as: "A multidisciplinary science that seeks to understand both the intimate mechanisms of aging and its etiopathogenesis. Its development as a science went through phases: the first one was merely empirical and speculative, drawing deductive conclusions and the second one is experimental, linked to the demonstration of its theories".

Gerontology maintains the contribution of different scientific disciplines that significantly support the result of research processes, whose aim is innovation, promotion, prevention and diagnosis of diseases that are immersed in areas of knowledge such as: social problems, psychological aspects, physiological bases, biological aspects and methodologies from other disciplines; medicine, anthropology and sociology.

GERIATRY

Nowadays, geriatrics is considered a branch of medicine that studies, prevents, diagnoses and treats the diseases of the elderly. The concept has evolved to consider a more comprehensive approach, which focuses not only on disease, but on the overall health of the older adult. Geriatrics deals with the clinical, preventive and social aspects of the disease in the elderly individual, and its main objective is to prevent and overcome the loss of autonomy, to which these people are particularly susceptible (Robles, 2001).

FINES PARTICULARES DE LA GERIATRÍA.	El desarrollo de un sistema asistencial a todos los niveles, que atienda las múltiples alteraciones y los problemas médico-sociales de los ancianos, que de forma aguda y postaguda presentan como rasgos comunes la pérdida de su independencia física o social.
	La organización de una asistencia prolongada a los ancianos que la necesiten.
	La movilización de todos los recursos para integrar en la comunidad el mayor número de ancianos posible.
	La investigación, la docencia y la formación continuada de sus propios especialistas y del personal relacionado con dicha especialidad.

DIFFERENCES BETWEEN GERIATRICS AND GERONTOLOGY

Geriatrics is part of gerontology, being a specialization within the medical sciences in charge of the diagnosis, treatment and prevention of medical problems associated with aging (Valencia, 2019). When considering geriatrics a common doubt is the differentiation with gerontology. Geriatrics deals with the study of the aging process as a whole, not only from a biomedical point of view, but rather from a general point of view. On the other hand, gerontology deals with the study and/or intervention in areas such as social, psychological, anthropological and even philosophical. Gerontology is considered to include geriatrics, but is not limited to it.

COMPREHENSIVE CARE

It is an intervention aimed at older adults, with an approach that addresses all the needs of the patient completely, and not only medical and physical needs, but also those that include promotion, prevention, recovery and rehabilitation activities at three levels: individual, family and community. (PAHO, 1980). Integrated care is a type of intervention aimed at older adults, providing a range of environments that benefit the processes of intervention, focused on the needs of each user, as well as strengthening and supporting the technical capacity of the services that the older adult should receive. Since 1980, the specific areas of action that PAHO has prioritized in its recommendations for the formulation of health programs and services for the elderly are

PROGRAMAS COMUNITARIOS INTEGRALES

Proporcionan una gama de entornos para el envejecimiento sano, y programas concebidos para apoyar las actividades de cuidado familiar, la protección de la dignidad de las personas y evitar el internamiento innecesario en establecimientos asistenciales cuya salud ambiental es frágil.

PROGRAMAS FORMULADOS

Fortalece la capacidad técnica de los servicios socio-sanitarios para las personas adultas mayores.

PROGRAMAS CONCEBIDOS

Ofrece incentivos capaces de alentar la autonomía, las actividades socialmente productivas y los programas generadores de ingresos para las personas adultas mayores.

LIFE STANDARDS

Nowadays, talking about quality of life, refers to a concept that sustains diverse levels that can visualize biological, economic, social and psychological demands in individual form up to the community level, related to several aspects of social welfare. According to the (WHO, 2015)The "perception of an individual's place in existence in the context of the culture and value system in which he lives and in relation to his goals, expectations, norms and concerns". Therefore, what we call quality of life brings together objective and subjective elements of social welfare that are founded on experience, whether individual or communal, within social life.

AGING

A gradual process that develops during the course of life and that involves biological, physiological, psychosocial and functional changes, which are associated with dynamic and permanent interactions between the subject and his environment. From a biological point of view, ageing is the consequence of the accumulation of a wide variety of molecular and cellular damage over time, leading to a gradual decline in physical and mental capacities, an increased risk of disease, and ultimately death. (WHO, 2018).

HEALTHY AGING

It is the process of fostering and maintaining functional capacity that enables well-being in old age. With this new concept, healthy aging does not mean aging without disease. Healthy aging means being able to do the things we value for as long as possible. (PAHO, Pan American Health Organization, 2019)

Healthy aging is a chain by which the older adult has reached a stage where he sees as a result the whole process of the factors that influenced in the course of his life, showing optimal results in all its aspects, nutritional, physical and cognitive.

ACTIVE AGEING

It is the process by which opportunities for physical, social and mental well-being are optimized throughout life, with the aim of extending healthy life expectancy, productivity and quality of life in old age. This definition not only looks at ageing from the perspective of health care, but also incorporates all the factors in the social, economic and cultural areas that affect the ageing of people (WHO, 2010). Active aging is a fundamental means of reaching the significant potential in the full enjoyment of life, focused on the state of health, physical, mental and autonomy, oriented to the promotion and prevention of diseases to improve their quality of life.

GERONTOGERIATRIC ASSESSMENT

The gerontogeriatric evaluation is one of the tools that the Social Worker must supervise before being synthesized, it is a multifunctional and dimensional diagnosis that demonstrates the result of a whole intervention processed by the interdisciplinary team, which must be applied every three months by quarters, for its application an excellent work team is needed, and this one is formed by the Clinical Psychologist, Occupational Therapist, Physical Therapist and the Social Worker; This last one is in charge of the application, evaluation and realization of a general report known as "Social Screening", which is an x-ray in social terms, because it shows all kind of information related to the individual intervention plans that each professional made. . In other words, it studies the older adult in all his potential, focusing on his areas of study to prioritize his needs based on the results obtained. Laforest (1991) defines it as: "the study of the old age from an interdisciplinary approach, being its purpose to know the process of aging for the application of tests of evaluations in the professional practice that allows to improve the quality of life of the old adults".

INTEGRAL INDIVIDUAL INTERVENTION PLAN (PIII)

The PIII is a specific planning made by each professional of the interdisciplinary team, this is done individually, that is, by each user, in this case older adults. Before considering the application plan with activities directed to the user, the Social Worker together with the interdisciplinary team must clarify objectives, establish goals and consider the abilities and weaknesses of the older adult, since each user is different, it is a different world and deserves an intervention with a spirit of service to improve their condition based on autonomy.

SOCIAL SCREENING

Social screening also known as "rapid screening" is the evaluation of the older adult in all its magnitude or capacity, is the result of all the interventions, assessments, evaluation, plans and programs carried out by the professionals of the interdisciplinary team. Zimmermman (2011) states that: "Social screening in the elderly is the multidimensional and usually interdisciplinary diagnostic process aimed at quantifying in functional terms the medical, mental and social capacities and problems of the elderly with a view to developing a plan for promotion, prevention, care or rehabilitation, as appropriate". Social screening considers the comprehensive care that the older adult receives, among other factors that affect his or her development within the gerontological center to improve the aging process.

FUNCTIONS OF THE SOCIAL WORKER IN GERONTOLOGICAL CENTRES

The functions of the Social Worker in the Gerontological Centers vary from the institutional and professional perspective, among them they must obtain a preliminary evaluation of the users before putting together their file, make social reports with the due recommendations, make home visits in case they have a family member and try to get the older adult involved and reinserted in their daily activities. One of the most outstanding tasks is to collaborate in the readaptation and rehabilitation of the elderly, accompanied by the technical team to improve their living conditions.

<table>
<tr><td>FUNCIONES
PRINCIPALES</td><td>Evaluación preliminar de las personas adultas mayores, que solicitan el ingreso al centro residencial a través de la aplicación de fichas sociales.</td></tr>
<tr><td></td><td>Procurar la reinserción de la persona adulta mayor a su núcleo familiar.</td></tr>
<tr><td></td><td>Participar con el equipo multidisciplinario en la evaluación de a persona adulta mayor, en igual forma en la organización, programación y evaluación de las diversas actividades del centro residencial.</td></tr>
<tr><td></td><td>Realizar visitas domiciliarias a las personas adultas mayores y emitir el informe social con las debidas recomendaciones.</td></tr>
<tr><td></td><td>Colaborar en la readaptación y rehabilitación psíquica y física de las personas adultas mayores.</td></tr>
<tr><td></td><td>Acompañar al equipo técnico en la observación, abordaje e intervención que se realiza en calle para realizar la intervención social, para la atención a personas adultas mayores en situación de calle.</td></tr>
<tr><td></td><td>Realizar la identificación, mapeo y coordinación de redes institucionales, sociales y/o familiares, que habiliten una salida de las personas adultas mayores en situación de calle.</td></tr>
<tr><td></td><td>Realizar coordinación interinstitucional para mejorar las condiciones de vida de las personas adultas mayores en situación de calle.</td></tr>
</table>

THE ROLE OF THE SOCIAL WORKER IN BASIC GENERAL EDUCATION CENTRES

Today's society presents new and disturbing challenges in the task of training and orienting for life; the Ecuadorian education system has sought to reconfigure itself around these demands; ascribing guidelines that the State, the Constitution, the Organic Law on Intercultural Education (LOEI) and its Regulations pose as the legal and political framework for disseminating quality education. This vision seeks to break the status-quo that prevailed in the traditional education system with its respective limitations, and to promote a new model that ensures comprehensive training that meets conditions of free education, equal opportunities, inclusion and participation, respect for diversity and freedoms, as well as the protection of children and adolescents. In this sense, education must be conceived as an essential component of Good Living and a priority area of public policy, promoting a model centered on human beings and their social and natural environment, considering the preparation of future citizens for a more democratic, equitable, inclusive, peaceful society, promoting interculturalism, diversity and respect for nature.

In this case, the Social Worker, based on the competences established by the LOEI and the technical support of routes and protocols of internal institutional regulations, the educational function is born, this refers to the problems that have to be faced in the educational family. Over time, the Social Worker has carried out activities such as socioeconomic studies for the correct provision of specific institutional services, palliative actions and has provided immediate benefits. In most cases, he has neglected the educational function, which has been systematically applied. This function implies an instruction, training or coaching to achieve the much desired change of attitudes (in persons or groups), which go from the static and therefore expectant to an attitude that motivates positive and participatory actions.

This approach requires the Social Worker to carry out an educational task, as a specific action to be developed based on the objectives and goals set. The Social Worker is essentially an educator at an individual, group or community work level, who uses formal and informal techniques to lead the social group to training and promotion of self-management and learning. For this purpose, the Student Counselling Departments were created, which used to be called "guidance department", with the sole purpose of focusing transcendently on situations presented in the educational community with a specific intervention approach for promotion, prevention, empowerment and the development of activities that stimulate and improve the student's stay, creating a connection between the educator and the student.

Once the human being is recognized as an integral system, which is configured by variables such as physical, cognitive, emotional and relational development of participation, values and principles, the process of accompaniment and counseling will become the link that consolidates being, knowing and doing. On the other hand, it is important to note that the human being develops in a macro system such as society, which has a set of historical and cultural patterns that are transmitted from generation to generation. Society in turn is made up of different environments or microsystems that are interrelated with each other, in which the human being develops and interacts with other people, acquiring the same values, habits, beliefs, skills, etc.

STUDENT DEVELOPMENT ENVIRONMENTS

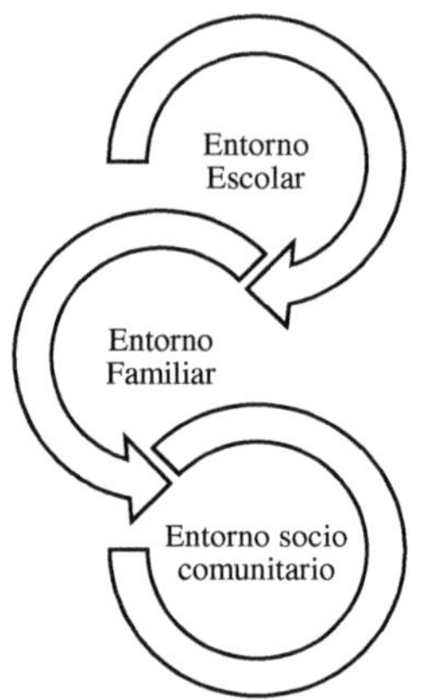

SCHOOL ENVIRONMENT

The school environment has to be configured in such a way as to approximate a "simulation cockpit" which, although different from the adult environment in social life and at work, has put in place all the necessary elements so that the "flight" towards autonomy does not lead to frustration. Normally, the vital test for which the school environment has to be prepared is subject to regulation, i.e., as in fair play, there are also regulations to be respected. Spranger (1964) He states that "In any case, the school environment can have no other purpose than to support the supreme goal of the school: the general formation of man crowned by the ethical-religious idea: "to develop and strengthen systematically, on the basis of its own elements, all the intrinsic forces of the child, his thought, feeling and will".

FAMILY CIRCLE

When we speak of family environment we refer to those people who live together, united by a biological or adoptive bond, which created among them a community of mutual affection and protection. Without a doubt, the family environment conditions the people who are part of it, according to the ties that are generated there. A child born into a family with very limited economic resources, with absent parents, without appropriate care, will have an inappropriate environment, whose fabric will generate a context, the significance of which will negatively influence that person in formation; on the contrary, a child who grows up in a family environment surrounded by affection and with his or her material needs satisfied and with the limits reasonably imposed, will have an environment that predisposes him or her to a healthy adulthood. The family environment can favour or destabilise the process of teaching and learning in the student, which is why the family plays a very important role in the development of the student's qualities, whether it is due to situations that arise in the course of his school life. Moral, family and emotional support to get out of his comfort zone is of great help.

SOCIO-COMMUNITY ENVIRONMENT

It is one that brings together all the institutions whose purpose is to develop and facilitate social, academic and personal skills, with the aim of improving the quality of life. Here we consider important observation points in the development of the student body, such as:

- Children at risk

- People in rehabilitation

- Levelling of studies

- Organizational work

- Vocational guidance

Here the Social Worker should implement a work plan, either individual or group as the situation warrants, to promote efforts in the prevention of future situations or scenarios unfavorable to the student.

APPROACHES TO THE DECD MODEL

The operating model of the Student Counselling Departments (DECE) is based on the approaches of law, gender, welfare, intergenerational, intercultural, inclusion and pedagogical, premises that are cross-cutting by the general principles established in the LOEI, article 2, as philosophical, conceptual and constitutional foundations that support, define and govern decisions and activities in the field of education. In order for DECE professionals to implement plans, programmes and projects, consideration has been given to configuring a management model that is implemented through recognition of the above-mentioned approaches, conceptual assumptions that make it possible to build a comprehensive vision of individual and collective development.

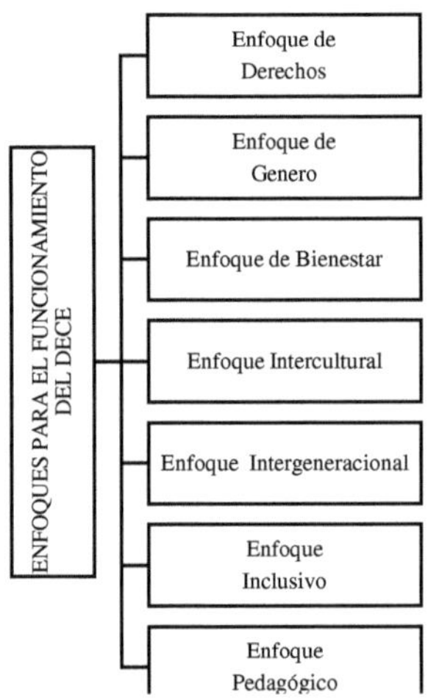

Prepared by: Author
Source: National Directorate of Education

These approaches imply a subjective relationship based on the aspirations of the institution and the individual perspectives of each student, with the aim of promoting integral human development from a rights, gender, welfare, intercultural, intergenerational and inclusion approach to achieve participation, permanence and completion of academic studies, ensuring their personal, social and emotional development within the institution.

PROFESSIONAL COMPETENCE OF THE SOCIAL WORKER

a) Knowledge of the Constitution of the Republic, the National Plan for Good Living, the Code for Children and Adolescents, the Organic Law on Intercultural Education, the Regulations to the LOEI, the Disabilities Law, the Regulations to the Disabilities Law, Ministerial Agreements, the Organic Law on Higher Education (LOES), the Regulations to the National System of Equalization and Admission (SNNA) and other regulations, plans, programmes and social policies concerning children and adolescents.

(b) knowledge and application of psychological, neurological and pedagogical principles in the scientific approach to problems and variables linked to behavioural and learning problems

(c) Knowledge and application of the fundamentals of general and educational psychology, evaluation

educational, human development, attention in contexts of diversity, psycho-educational intervention, learning theories, teaching-learning methodologies, personal, academic, vocational and professional orientation theories, personality theories, educational inclusion and construction of life projects.

(d) Knowledge and application of strategies to identify the main problems affecting children and young people, and application of tools for the peaceful resolution of conflicts and mediation techniques

(e) Knowledge and application of counselling techniques and methods that facilitate personal, group and family decision-making in the context of building life projects.

f) Knowledge and application of participatory techniques and group processes that promote personal and collective empowerment.

g) Implements strategies that promote student participation in preventive and life skills development plans, programs and projects

h) Management of planning processes, design and execution of research projects, analysis and educational approach.

PROFESSIONAL CAPACITY

The professional in Social Work must have certain characteristics necessary in the development of any activity related to the educational area, that is why the professional has to be capable in various scenarios that are immersed in the school society, among them must have:

- Expresión escrita
- Capacidad de análisis
- Identificación de problemas y dificultades
- Comunicación efectiva
- Capacidad para identificar consecuencias a los antecedentes
- Juicio crítico en la toma de decisiones
- Pensamiento Crítico
- Planificador
- Capacidad de Gestión
- Trabajo en equipo
- Aprendizaje constante
- Orientación
- Actitud positiva

ATTITUDES

Here it is defined as the opinion that relates to the work of the profession in Social Work, in understanding adverse situations that involve a more focused and direct intervention. This attitude may have components related to psychology, sociology and anthropology, defining behaviors and actions that are sometimes aimed at student empowerment.

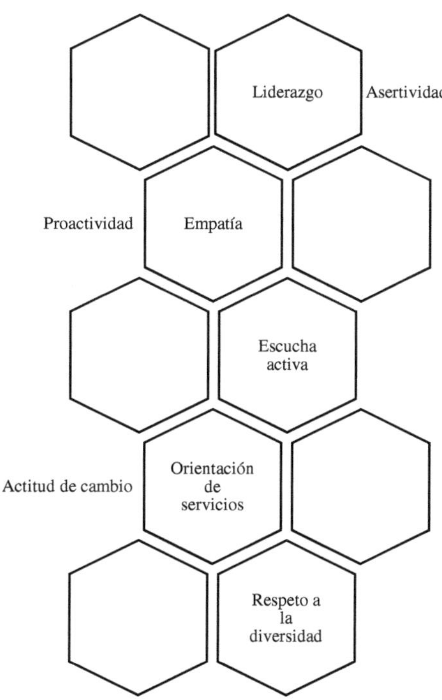

DEC STRUCTURE

In the case of educational institutions that have more than one day, the institutional educational authority must establish a flexible working schedule that makes it possible to cover the different days with the DECE service, taking into consideration the criterion of one professional for every 450 students in each day.

With regard to the organization and prioritization of work activities, DECE professionals will comply exclusively with the functions and procedures established in this model.

The Student Counseling Department will be made up of a team of professionals linked to profiles ranging from the Social Worker, Educational/Clinical Psychologist and Educational Counselor, one of whom will act as coordinator according to his or her experience and professional skills.

For the formation of DECE's team of professionals, it will be taken into consideration that the first and second professionals should be from the psychoeducational and inclusion support area, while the third professional may be from the social area. It should be stressed that, if the educational institution requires more than three professionals, the following profiles to be hired will be subject to institutional needs, always within the guidelines established in the present model.

FUNCTIONS OF THE SOCIAL WORKER IN THE DECD

The contribution of Social Work from the Student Counseling Department tends to focus on the area that investigates concrete processes related to the living conditions of individuals, their needs and potential; that intervenes in the recognition and resolution of problems between human and institutional interactions, in order to achieve greater social welfare; and that addresses methodologically the emerging contexts and dynamics that generate movements in society. Méndez (2018) The Social Worker in this area must display skills that allow him/her to consider cultures, symbolic representations, languages, interaction and communicative acts with and for the people he/she works with, so that he/she can execute forceful action and leave aside the palliative. Bearing in mind the factors linked to the family that affect the situation and performance of students in the school environment, as set out in the first chapter, and the sociocultural problems established in the model of comprehensive care: violence and/or sexual violence; the emergence and organization of gangs; trafficking and/or problematic consumption of alcohol, tobacco and other drugs; school dropouts due to child labour; trafficking in persons; and children and adolescents in situations of anger, among others".

According to (Gonzalez, 1993) In addition to those mentioned above, it includes participation, in collaboration with other professionals, in the development of support programmes such as the hospital classroom, care and guidance for health personnel and home care. In addition to the above-mentioned functions, it points out the following:

- Study the factors that in each case produce absenteeism, repetition, dropout and poor school performance.

- To serve as an intermediary between families, the school and school services for the proper diagnosis and treatment of various forms of school maladjustment, as well as for school and vocational guidance.

- To inform about the socioeconomic status of the families applying for scholarships or grants.

- To study with the appropriate techniques the social, economic and cultural problems that facilitate the comparison of school action plans.

- To carry out activities corresponding to the "public relations" of the school in order to accredit it and root it in social control.

It is not the same to generate a direct action of prevention than of attention, that is why the functions of the Social Worker, based on the abilities acquired in the academic learning process, show an almost invisible role in the professional action, since they guarantee the right to education of the students, showing it as a main actor between the school/school and the family.

BIBLIOGRAPHY

U.S. National Academy of Sciences (March 21, 2018). Retrieved from https://www.universidadviu.com/gerontologia-definicion/

Castellanos, M. (1993). *Manual de Trabajo Social.* Mexico: Profasr.

Gonzalez, E. (1993). *Education and Social Work.* Retrieved from file:///C:/Users/MARITZA%20FARFAN/Downloads/Dialnet-AnalisisDeFuncionesDelTrabajadorSocialEnElCampoEdu-2002450%20(6).pdf.

LAFOREST, J. (1991). *INTRODUCTION TO GERONTOLOGY.* BARCELONA: HERDER.

Organic Law of the Elderly. (2019). Quito: National.

Mendez, V. (June 30, 2018). *Social Work and Primary Education.* Retrieved from https://www.eumed.net/rev/caribe/2018/07/trabajador-social-consejeria.html#:~:text=The%20port%20of%20work%20Social,individuals%2C%20your%20needs%20and%20potentials.&text=The%20work%20social%20is%20tan,environment%20in%20the%20that%20intervenes.

WHO. (20 JUNE 2010). *ACTIVE AGING IN THE COMPREHENSIVE DEVELOPMENT OF OLDER ADULTS.* Retrieved from https://www.hola.com/salud/enciclopedia-salud/2010062045408/mayores/generales/envejecimiento-activo-y-saludable/

WHO. (14 June 2013). *World Health Organization.* Retrieved from http://preventivaysocial.webs.fcm.unc.edu.ar/files/2014/04/Unidad-5-Salud-Adulto-Mayor-V-2013.

WHO. (15 February 2015). Retrieved from https://www.uaeh.edu.mx/scige/boletin/prepa2/n2/m2.html#:~:text=Si%20tomamos%20en%20concuenta%20el,expectativas%2C%20normas%20y%20sus%20inquietudes.

WHO. (2018). *INTER-AMERICAN CONVENTION ON THE RIGHTS OF THE ELDERLY.*

OPS. (1980). *PAN AMERICAN HEALTH ORGANIZATION FOR OLDER ADULTS.* TECHNICAL STANDARD .

OPS. (2019). *Pan American Health Organization.* Retrieved from https://www.paho.org/hq/index.php?option=com_content&view=article&id=13634:healthy-aging&Itemid=42449&lang=es

Piña, M. (2004). *GERONTOLOGICAL SOCIAL WORK.* BUENOS AIRES: ESPACIO.

Robles, M. J. (2001). *DEFINITION AND OBJECTIVES OF GERIATRICS.* Barcelona: Llorach.

Spranger, E. (1964). *Educational Pedagogy.* Marseille: Meyer.

Valencia. (March 26, 2019). *Concepts and differences between Geriatrics and Gerontology.* Retrieved from https://www.universidadviu.com/que-es-geriatria/

Zimmermman, J. (2011). *MEDICAL GUIDE FOR COMPREHENSIVE CARE IN THE ELDERLY.* PANAMA: DONDERIS.

Printed by Books on Demand GmbH, Norderstedt / Germany